Usborne
Phonics Readers
Ted in a red bed

Phil Roxbee Cox

Illustrated by Stephen Cartwright

Edited by Jenny Tyler

Language consultant: Marlynne Grant
BSc, CertEd, MEdPsych, PhD, AFBPs, CPsychol

There is a little yellow duck to spot in every picture.

First published in 2006 by Usborne Publishing Ltd., Usborne House, 83–85 Saffron Hill, London EC1N 8RT, England. www.usborne.com
Copyright © 2006, 1999 Usborne Publishing Ltd.

Ted likes to shop.

Ted stops. Ted hops.
Ted smiles a big smile.

"I like this bed," thinks Ted.

"I like red wood. Red wood is good."

"I want to see more."

He goes into the

"Try the red bed," says Fred.

"Oh, yes," says Ted.

Ted slips
his feet
under
the sheet.

He flops on the pillow.

The pillow is yellow.

"I need this bed, Fred!" grins Ted.

"It is a nice price," smiles Fred.

Now it's Ted's bed, not Fred's bed.

Ted feels sleepy.
Ted falls asleep.

Ted has a dream.

He bobs down a stream.

Ted has a dream.

He bobs on a wave

into a cave.

Ted has a dream.

He can
fly in the sky!

Ted has a dream.
He is back by the stream.

Ted wakes up with a snore.

He's not in the store any more.

Ted is home. His bed is home too.

"This red bed must be a magic red bed!"